AF231040

Dedication

To the fabulous girls in my life,
Carlie Louise and Laura Leigh,
the best daughters a mother could ever wish for.

To my special, beautiful grand-daughters
Cloe Maria and Shayla Nicole.

To my Mum, Eve Maria Ring and Sister Karen Annette
for showing me love and support.

I wish you colourful happy lives and may your true colours
always shine brightly.

Colour In My World

CONTENTS

CHAPTER THREE

CHAPTER FOUR

CHAPTER FIVE

CHAPTER SIX

CHAPTER SEVEN

Introduction

We live in a colourful world. Colour is EVERYWHERE ! From the moment we wake up to the time we go to bed, it is there for all to see – and even sometimes in our dreams. Whether you take it for granted or are fascinated by it, colour is continually having an effect on you. Throughout the history of the world light and colour have been thought of as essential for good health and well-being. Quite simply, it feeds our mind, body and spirit.

This book is about colour and you. You'll be looking at your own colouring and how to find your colour sign.

Many famous artists have known that blending some colours can bring them to life, while other combinations clash and just don't look right. It's the same with us. We all have colours in our hair, skin and eyes and there are many fascinating colours to complement your own unique colouring. You'll be wearing different colours all your life - so why not start to discover the best ones for you now? The colours that suit you will light up your face, help you to feel confident and allow your personality to shine through.

You can learn to use colour to help you have more fun, comfort you, energise and relax you. It's like having your very own colour toolbox. Once you get to know the colours in your toolbox you can take various ones out and use them for your benefit whenever you choose.

Get ready for fun and creativity on a colourful trip throughout this book. For some of the activities included you will need paints, coloured pencils and paper.

CHAPTER ONE

Mirror, mirror on the wall...

...who's the fairest of them all ?

When I was eight years old, my friend and I were playing and dressing up in front of the mirror.

We looked so different from one another. Fiona had brown-black hair, clear blue eyes and pale skin. Her colouring looked like Snow White.

In contrast my hair was light brown, my eyes green-brown and my skin a rosy pink. I remember thinking how lovely she looked.

Why did I look so washed out and faded compared to Fiona ?

I had no idea at that time that the colours I wore close to my face make such a difference to how I looked and felt about myself. I did, however, have a favourite lavender dress. I loved that dress ! I felt so special when I wore it. If only I'd known as a child which colours suited me best, I could've looked fantastic all the time. I would have felt great in everything, not to mention how easy it would have been in my teenage years and beyond when choosing and buying my own clothes.

Many years later, I learnt that there are various palettes of colour to help everyone feel their best and suit their colouring.

I discovered my colouring is flattered by soft dusty colours like blue grey, dusty pink, soft yellow and of course lavender.

Darker stronger colours are too overpowering for me and make me look very pale, while golden warm colours make me look totally unwell.

Looking back I realised that Fiona's colouring was much stronger; it's no wonder she looked fantastic in clear bright colours.

What's your colouring ?

Understanding your colouring

Our skin tone, eye colour and hair colour each have their own undertones which make up our personal colouring.

We have inherited our colouring from our relatives, passed down through our family genes. Just like mixing paints, our genes have combined to create our own unique colouring.

You are the fairest of them all because Nature doesn't make mistakes. We all have lovely coloured eyes, hair and skin which harmonise perfectly and naturally.

If you have a really good look at your colouring it will be easier to find your sign and discover the colours that bring out the best in you.

You will need:

- A mirror

- Good daylight

- A friend or family member to help you

If possible, sit outside or near a window.
Daylight is the best light to see the colour of your skin, hair and eyes most clearly.
Now let's have a good look.

What colours do you see in your :

Skin........................

There are lots of different colours in people's skin.
Do you have freckles? Is your skin pink, golden, peachy, beige, very dark or very pale ?

Put a photo of yourself here!

Eyes........................

Can you see more than one colour ?
Do your eyes have little dots of different colours, called flecks ?
Some children have a ring around their eye colour or feather patterns.
Describe the colour - for example, if your eyes are blue, are they bright, light or turquoise ?

Hair........................

Is your hair light or dark ? Is it all one colour ? Does it have grey, golden or red tones ?

Colouring..................

What is the overall look of your skin/eyes/hair ?
Bright, clear, soft, rosy, golden, warm, deep, cool or fair ?

Fun Activity

Here's an activity for you to do. Help a friend to discover their colouring.

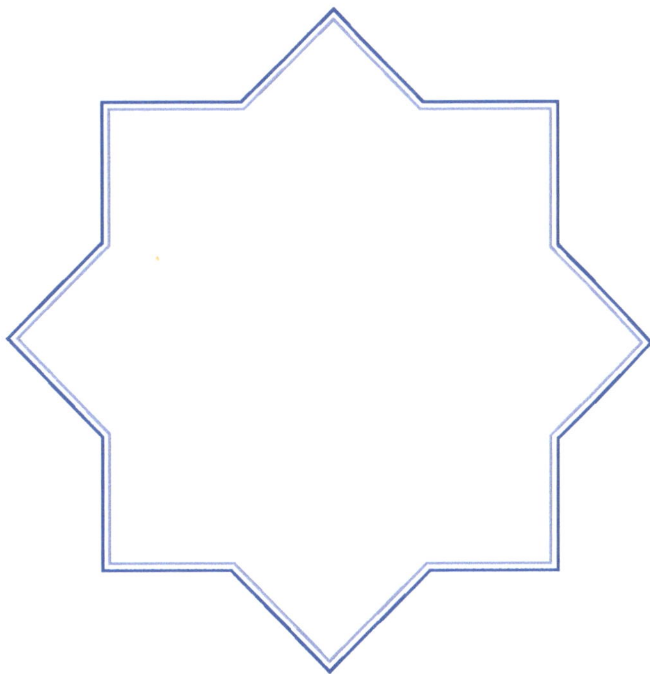

Fix a photo to the star or draw a picture of your friend.
What colours do you see in their :

Skin..........................

Eyes..........................

Hair..........................

Now you've had a good look at your own and your friend's colouring, let's do the Colour Test.

 # Colour Test 

Let's see which colours look best on you.

This is going to be fun !

If you want you could have a Colour Test party with your friends. You'll need:

- to wear a white or pale coloured top
- lots of coloured items, including different shades of the same colour

Remember to ask permission to borrow things like clothes, scarves, towels, pillow cases, coloured paper, material or anything colourful that isn't too big.
When you've done this you're ready to begin.

You're going to try on all the colours you've gathered - one at a time, of course !
Just because you like a colour, it doesn't always mean it will suit you. You want people to notice how great you look, not just the colours you're wearing.

Look in the mirror and put a coloured item under your chin and across your chest. Compare orange with pink, brown with blue, white with cream.
Try different reds and greens. Do you look better in silver or gold ?

This is where other people can help you by telling you what they think.

Ask yourself these questions:

1) Do I feel good in this colour ?

2) Does the colour light up my face ?

3) Do I look healthy in this colour ?

If your answer was yes to all these questions, put the item on your 'Best Colours' pile. If you answered no, put it on another pile.
Go through all of the colours until you finish with two piles.
Now look at the items in your 'Best Colours' pile.
Colour in the four stars in the colours you like most.

This will help you to find your colour sign.

Are you .... SUN, MOON, SEA or EARTH ?

CHAPTER TWO

What's My Colour Sign ?

The four colour signs

SUN

MOON

SEA

EARTH

Now that you've taken a good look at your colouring and completed the colour test, you should have an idea of your colouring and some of the colours that suit you. There are four major signs with palettes of colours to suit everyone's colouring.

Look at the pictures of children on the following pages.

To find your colour sign, try to see which of them have colours in the skin, hair and eyes that are most like yours.

The Sun Sign

In the soft blue sky are the sun's rays,

Summer fun and happy days,

Pastel kites gently floating by,

Strawberry and vanilla ice cream, my oh my.

Sun Sign

Sun Sign colouring

All the Sun children have soft, rosy and cool colouring.

Skin

Rosy pink
Ivory
Beige
Pink beige

Eyes

Soft brown or blue
Soft grey or green
Brown-green
Clear blue
Blue-green
Blue brown
Cloudy
White flecks
Grey circle around them

Hair

Silver-blonde
Light-dark blonde
Mousey brown
Dark brown
Light brown

Sun Sign colours

My sun sign colours are soft, cool and blended.

My white is a soft white. I can wear lots of blues except the very strong ones. I can wear pinky brown and beige, blue-grey, soft navy, soft yellow, apple green, blue-green, sky blue, soft purple, mauve, lavender, plum, burgundy, raspberry, sherbet pink, strawberry and watermelon red.

Colours to avoid:
Black, pure white, orange, orange-red, gold, yellow-green, gold, rust, golden brown and very strong colours.

Tip: If your colouring is fair, wear the lighter colours near to your face. Wear the stronger colours if your colouring is darker.

Sun Sign Colour Chart

The Moon Sign

I see the moon and the moon sees me,

Sparkling space ships fill me with glee,

Ribbons of clear, silvery light,

Shining all around, chasing the night.

Moon Sign

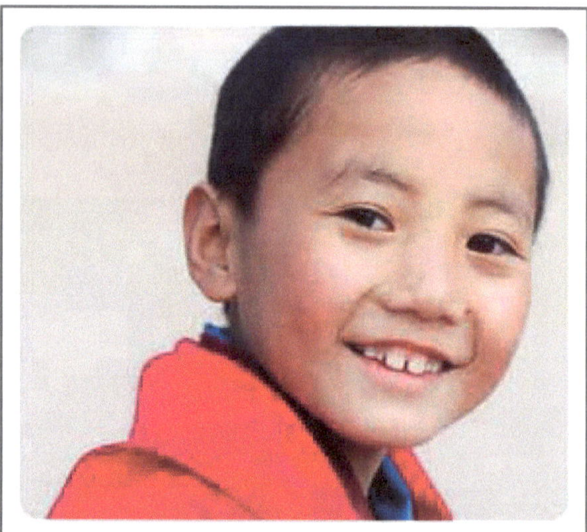

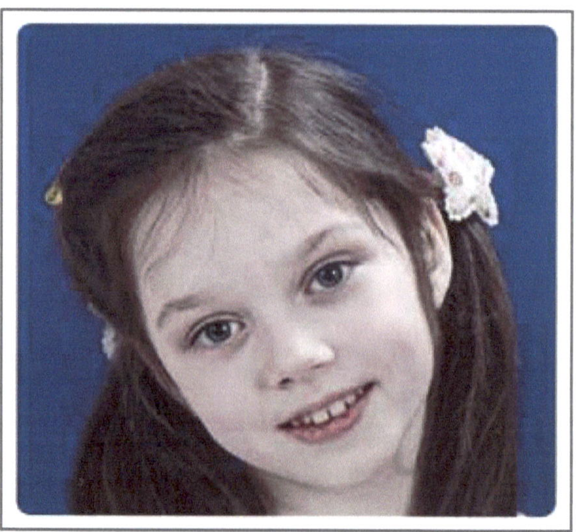

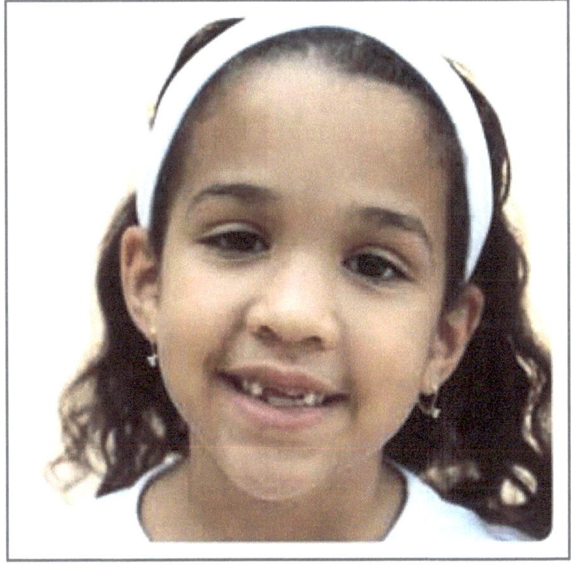

Moon Sign colouring

All the Moon children have strong, clear and deep colouring.

Skin

Milky white
Beige
Dark brown
Olive
Cocoa brown
Black

Eyes

Clear blue
Violet-blue
Grey or green brown
Dark green
Dark brown
Grey circle around the iris
White flecks

Hair

White-blonde
Light, medium or dark brown
Dark red-brown
Black

Moon Sign colours

My moon sign colours are vivid, clear and cool.

I can wear black and brilliant white. Grey, lemon yellow, strong blue, dark navy and turquoise – these are all great on me. I can mix them with hot pink, strong purple, burgundy, clear blue-red, emerald and pine green. I can wear all my colours in icy shades (white with a hint of colour) like icy violet, icy green, icy grey, icy blue, icy aqua. I can combine these with my bold striking colours for lots of contrast, like icy pink with burgundy or icy green with emerald green……

Colours to avoid:
Orange, orange-red, golden brown, rust, yellow-green, gold, moss green and soft colours (pastels).

Tip: If your skin tone is very fair, mix light and dark colours near your face. Wear the stronger deeper colours if your colouring is darker.

Moon Sign Colour Chart

The Sea Sign

Children play with sea shells on the seashore,

Starfish, angelfish and bright things galore,

Orange crabs dancing hand in hand,

In between my toes, I feel the fine golden sand.

Sea Sign

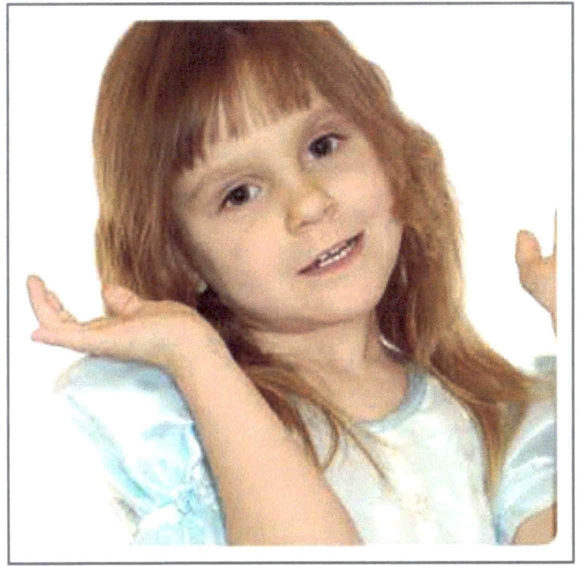
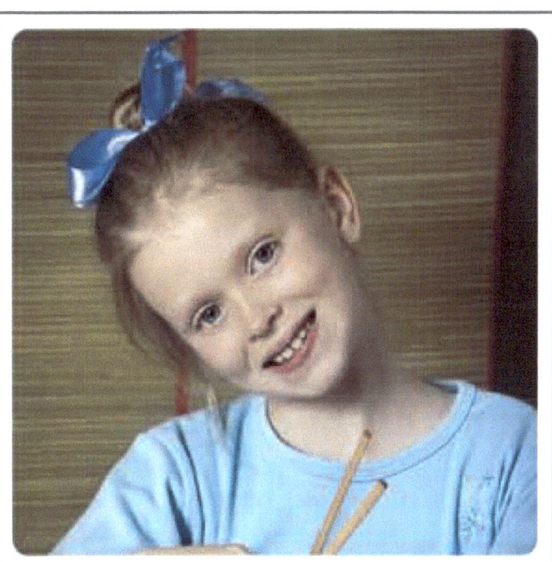

Sea Sign colouring

All the Sea children have delicate, clear and golden colouring.

Skin

Ivory
Soft beige
Peach
Golden with freckles

Eyes

Clear blue, green or brown
Violet-blue
Blue-green
Golden brown
Green-brown
Glass-like
White or golden flecks

Hair

Light blonde
Golden blonde
Copper
Light or medium brown
Red-brown

Sea Sign colours

My sea sign colours are clear, lively and warm.

My best white is sea shell or ivory. I can wear beige, clear gold, sand, bright golden yellow and golden brown. Bright sea blues from aqua to turquoise, ocean navy and clear violet are also in my colour range. I look good in dolphin grey, warm shell pink, salmon pink, orange coral and seaweed yellow green. My reds are bright lobster and crab orange-red.

Colours to avoid:
Cool pink, pale lavender, olive green, and burgundy. Pure white, black and dark or dusty colours.

Tip: If you are very fair, you can wear a lighter tint of pink and look good in the lighter colours in your sign near to your face. If your hair is more golden and your colouring is stronger, wear the brighter warmer colours close to your face.

Sea Sign Colour Chart

The Earth Sign

A treasure chest full of shimmering gold,

The earth's secrets are waiting to be told,

Forests of towering, rich green trees,

Crispy, colourful, changing Autumn leaves.

Earth Sign

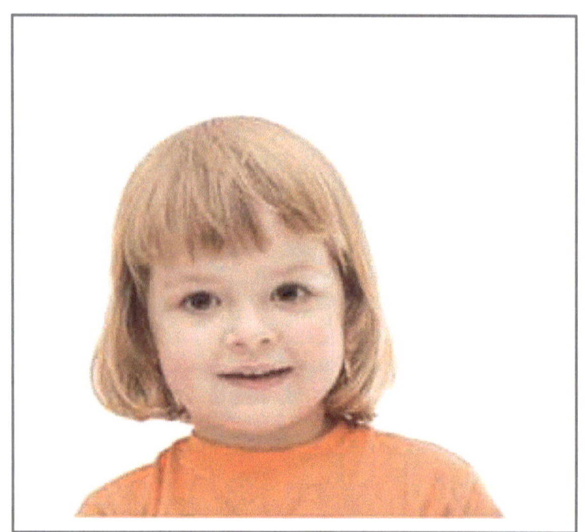

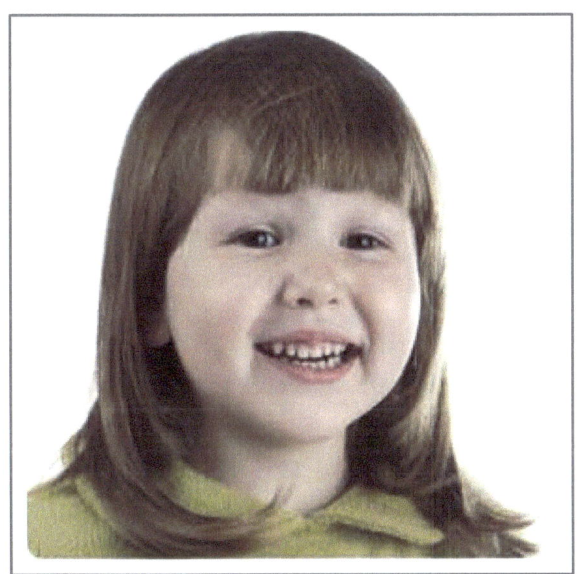

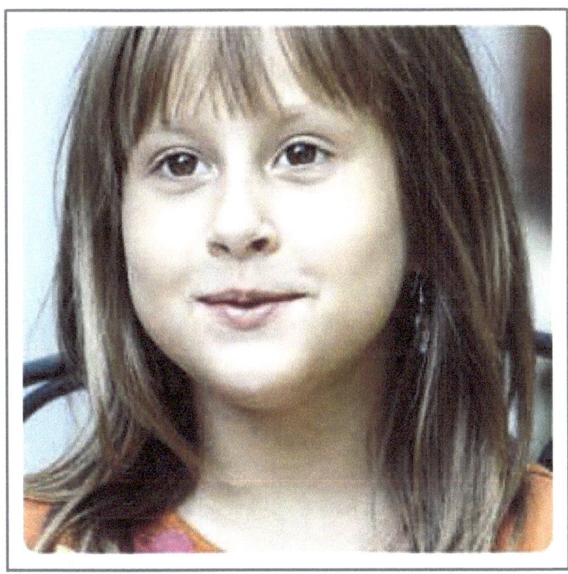

Earth Sign colouring

All the Earth children have golden, rich and warm colouring.

Skin

Fair
Warm beige
Honey
Golden brown
Olive
Bronze
Golden brown freckles

Eyes

Golden brown
Warm green
Brown
Blue-green
Gold feathers or brown flecks

Hair

Golden blonde
Red
Copper
Light, medium or dark brown

Earth Sign colours

My earth sign colours are earthy, warm and rich

My colours are creamy white, earth-browns, beige, camel, coffee, rust and mahogany. I can wear gold, pumpkin, mango, deep apricot, peach, terracotta, mustard and golden yellow. I have many greens to choose from, like forest, olive and moss green. My blues are soft turquoise, blue-green (teal), purple, navy-green and I can wear all reds with warm tones such as tomato red, orange-red and brick red.

Colours to avoid:
Black, white, grey, burgundy red and all cool light pastel colours.

Tip: If your colouring is fair, wear the softer, lighter colours close to your face. If your colouring is darker wear the brighter colours. If you have warm skin with freckles, then golden rich earthy colours will be great close up to your face.

Earth Sign Colour Chart

Colours we can all wear

Go ahead - wear them !

These colours can be worn by all the signs as they are neither too cool nor too warm and so look wonderful on all skin tones. They suit everybody.

To get the most benefit from wearing your colours, it is much better to wear natural fibres like cotton. Natural material lets the light filter through and allows the skin to breathe so the body can absorb the colour. This makes a big difference to how we feel when we are wearing our colours. It is also more comfortable to wear natural material as it helps us to perspire less.

School

The colour of uniforms encourages us to be neat and tidy. They are usually dark green, blue, grey, black or brown.

If your school lets you, why not dress it up with your sign colours ?

You can use your own ideas to express your personality, but here are some for you to try.

- Wearing a coat or jacket in your favourite colour
- Hat, scarf and gloves in your sign colours
- Hair bands and ties
- Bag and pencil case

Even if you are not allowed, you can always wear coloured underwear. Ha ha !

Remember that wearing yellow is good for concentration and may help you at school.

When the day is over and it's time to change out of your uniform, get comfortable in your favourite relaxed colour to feel free to express your own personality.

If you don't wear a uniform and can wear your own choice of colours – lucky you !

CHAPTER THREE

Dress It Up

We can complement the way we look and even turn something plain into something amazing by adding a few accessories. The items you choose to dress it up also reflect your personality and individual style. This chapter has lots of information for girls, but there may be some interesting nuggets for the boys too !

Accessory items like jewellery have a long and colourful history. Males and females used jewellery made from natural materials like gold, silver, gem stones, wood, animal teeth and shells to decorate themselves thousands of years ago.

Artistic designs today are inspired from our ancestors and from different cultures, while the materials used come from all over the world.

There are over two hundred different types of gemstones alone, made from naturally occurring crystals in all the colours of the rainbow. They are valued not just for their beauty and colour but also their vibration and ability to create inner harmony.

All the more reason to wear them !

Accessory items include:

Shoes, bags, hats; earrings, watches, bracelets and pendants; chains and beads; rings, glasses and hair ornaments; belts, buckles, brooches, buttons, ties and scarves. The choices are endless.

Keep glitzy items for parties and looking your best and use casual less shiny items for dressing down days.

The size of your accessories will depend on you.

For example big earrings will look wrong if your face is small, and vice versa.

Friends and relatives love to buy accessory items for birthdays and special occasions, so if you follow the guide for your sign and make suggestions to help them choose the right gift idea for you, you'll be sure it's going to look right and make your outfit look just fabulous.

Accessory pieces are now being made with new inexpensive modern materials. This makes it possible for almost anyone to afford attractive jewellery. As some gemstones and mineral names come in a variety of colours only a few are suggested here for your Sign.

You can find similar items in glass and beads which are equally attractive, but use your colours as a guide.

Sun Sign

Choose:
Floral or blended designs.
Silver or soft coloured metallic or pearly finish.
Gemstones and minerals like citrine, kyanite, amethyst, blue lace agate, green aventurine, rose quartz and ruby. Soft white and pink tone pearls.

Shoes, bags and belts:
The basic neutrals which go with all of your Sun sign colours are:
Navy, blue-grey and soft brown. Silver, pewter or soft rose gold.
Soft white and light grey are great for the summertime.
Other colours are fine, if they match or blend with your clothes.

Moon Sign

Choose:
Bold or striking designs.
Silver or metallic finishes. Gemstones and minerals like diamond, emerald, clear quartz, white moonstone, sodalite, black obsidian, amethyst and garnet. Black or white pearls.

Shoes, bags and belts:
The basic neutrals which go with all of your Moon sign colours are:
Navy blue, black, grey and silver tones.
Stone, white and navy for the summertime.
Other colours are fine, if they match or blend with your clothes.

Sea Sign

Choose:
Delicate patterns and designs.
All light tones of gold. Ivory pearls and shell jewellery.
Gemstones and minerals like honey or peach calcite, red or cream coral, aquamarine, carnelian, amazonite and turquoise.

Shoes, bags and belts:
The basic neutrals which go with all of your Sea sign colours are:
Bright blue, light golden brown and light gold tones.
Shell white, cream and light golden sand in the summertime.
Other colours are fine if they match or blend with your clothes.

Earth Sign

Choose:
Rich and natural designs.
Bronze, copper, gold and brass tones.
Wooden beads in all the Earth sign colours. Cream pearls.
Gemstones and minerals like jade, natural agate, amber, yellow or red jasper, blue-green apatite and tiger's eye.

Shoes, bags and belts:
The basic colours which go with all your Earth sign colours are:
All shades of brown, dark green and gold tones.
Cream or light tan is great to wear in warmer weather.
You can wear other colours if they blend or match with your clothes.

CHAPTER FOUR

Colour In My World

Our magical world of colour is part of our everyday lives. Within every unique colour lie hidden benefits waiting to be discovered.

Good Vibrations

It's a scientific fact that everything in our world contains energy. Colours are a type of energy too - each colour has its own wavelength and vibrates at a different frequency.

Try to think of colours as music. Your ears pick up the vibrations of different musical notes and your eyes react to colour vibrations in a similar way. The coloured keyboard gives you an idea of how the colours vibrate.

Red vibrates slowly at one end of the spectrum and violet vibrates quickly at the other end of the spectrum.

The vibration of a colour is also absorbed through our skin and can affect us in many different ways. Colour can give us more energy or help us to feel relaxed. If we're feeling sad, it can even cheer us up.

Colours around you

We associate colour with many different things.
Try to think of more items which you associate with the different colours on the following pages.

Eye spy with my little eye something the colour of...

Red

♥ Red is the colour that stands out the most

♥ Wearing red can make you feel confident and help to give you more energy

♥ It's traditionally a warning colour

♥ When you wear red you'll want to be on the move and do things

♥ Red can help you to feel warm, so it's a good colour to wear in cold weather

Orange

♥ If you haven't been feeling well and not been eating properly, orange will help you get your appetite back

♥ Wear orange to a party. It's a fantastic colour for having lots of fun and laughter

♥ Orange lets your imagination run wild when you're doing art of any kind

♥ It can help you to feel positive about yourself

♥ If orange is not one of your colours you can always wear the colour salmon instead

Yellow

♥ Yellow is the brightest colour in the rainbow - it's the sunny, happy colour

♥ This colour can make you and those who see you wearing it smile

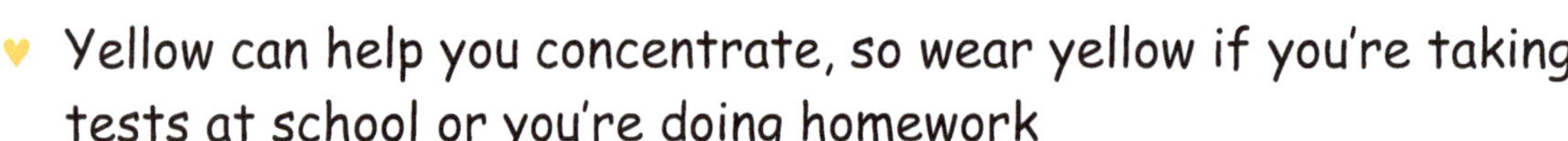

♥ Yellow can help you concentrate, so wear yellow if you're taking tests at school or you're doing homework

♥ Why not grow your own sun flowers ? Plant them in the Springtime to make a happy space in your garden

♥ Yellow may help with a nervous tummy and skin problems

Green

- ♥ It's the middle colour of the rainbow between yellow and blue. It's the colour of balance

- ♥ Green can help to ease a headache

- ♥ Green has a calming effect, so getting out and about in the countryside will make you feel relaxed

- ♥ Wear green to be caring and sharing with friends and the environment

- ♥ Wearing green can help you if you feel sick while travelling

Blue

♥ Blue is a peaceful, calm colour and can help you to chill out

♥ Blue may help you sleep

♥ Blue is a good healing colour, so wear it if you're not feeling well

♥ Wearing blue will help you to speak up for yourself and express your feelings

♥ If you have a fever, the vibration of blue can help to lower a high temperature

Indigo

♥ Indigo is the darkest colour in the rainbow and the most difficult to see. It can look almost black

♥ For a restful night, snuggle up in indigo pyjamas or bed covers

♥ It feels good to wear if someone has upset you, as it's a very comforting colour

♥ A colour of respect, often worn by adults as a uniform

♥ A mystical colour like the night sky. Helps you to go within yourself, to solve problems and make decisions

Violet

♥ When you wear violet, it can make you feel more in touch with your senses

♥ It's a good idea to have some lavender near to your bed. It's wonderfully soothing

♥ Wearing violet can help to distract you from any worries

♥ It's better to wear lighter tints or combine it with another colour, as it can be overwhelming to wear all day long on its own

♥ Wear it to be gentle with yourself and sensitive to others

Black and White

This ancient Eastern symbol is called a yin-yang symbol. Yin is black and yang is white. This represents the balance between two opposite forces such as female and male or darkness and light.

Black

Black is the opposite to white. It absorbs all of the other colours. It is thought to be mysterious and powerful - perhaps why it is a favourite with magicians and judges. Wear black if you're feeling vulnerable – it helps you to feel safe and protected and keeps people at a distance.

White

White feels fresh, clean, pure and positive – part of the reason why doctors and European brides traditionally wear white. It will help you to keep cool in warm weather because it contains all the colours in the spectrum and reflects the light.

It's not a good idea to wear too much black or white. They are very strong colours and can drain our energy. Remember that we all need variety in the colours we wear to help keep us in balance.

Unless you are a Moon sign, wearing these colours close to your face can make you look very pale. Wear black and pure white away from your face and add a splash of colour from your sign to make you look healthy and bring these colours to life.

The Colour Share Game

Believe it or not we experience colour through sound, touch, smell and even taste – not just sight ! We can enhance these senses just as someone who is born blind may have a heightened sense of hearing or touch (see page 85).

In this game, you're going to share your related thoughts and emotions about colour by using your different senses.
Here are a few examples of how you can connect a sense with a colour. However, the possibilities are endless.

1 Sight:
The easiest and most used. Simply picture anything in the chosen colour. **Yellow** could be the sunshine on a summer's day, an egg yolk or a duckling.

2 Hearing:
The world is full of sounds. **Blue** can conjure up thoughts of waves crashing in the sea. The sound of the wind whistling through the trees can connect you to the colour of the leaves. A chick chirping may trigger **yellow**, an image of orange juice may appear in your mind when you hear liquid being poured.

3 Touch:

The skin is the body's largest sensory organ. It is through the nerves on the skin that we get the feeling of touch. Describe the feeling you get from a colour. For example, you might say "**violet** feels soft and comforting, like my slippers" or "**red** feels cold and smooth like a tomato". You can use words like cold, soft, wet, slippery, bumpy, sticky etc.

4 Smell:

A smell often triggers memories, thoughts and feelings. It can also warn us if something is burning or if food smells bad. **Green** might remind you of the fresh scent of freshly-mown grass. Think of smells you can associate with colours.

5 Taste:

Taste is linked to smell. Words you might use to describe the sense of taste could be sweet, sour, bitter or salty. For example, the colour **indigo** might make you think of blackcurrant juice, so you may call indigo a sweet colour (or disgusting if you don't like blackcurrant juice !)

6 Intuition:

Often described as the sixth sense, intuition is a feeling, knowing or gut reaction. Sensing danger is a very common example and is often associated with **red. Blue** might make you feel very calm and secure without you really knowing why.

When playing the game, any reactions you have to colours are all great.
We're all different and colours have various meanings to all of us.

The Object of the Game

The first to finish linking all 10 colours to a sense is the winner.

To play the game you will need:

A dice and shaker
Counters
Minimum of 2 people
The Colour Game Board
Pen and paper
Timer (optional)

To Play:

Throw a dice to see who will go first, and then take turns.

1. Start with your counter on the Start Line and throw the dice. Counting Red as number 1, move the corresponding number of spaces clockwise. The colour you land on is the colour that you are going to connect with a sense.

2. Throw the dice again. Find the sense on the Senses List that matches the dice number. This is your sense to share.

3. Close your eyes to help you connect with your senses.

4. Share with the other players what the colour/sense combination means to you.

5. Make a note of the colours as you complete them.

6. If you throw a six, you can take another turn. Otherwise, finish your turn and hand the dice to the next player.

7. Miss a turn if you land on a colour for a second time.

8. To finish the game, you need to throw the correct number of spaces to land on your final colour. If you overshoot, keep moving around the circle again.

9. To win, you must connect all 10 colours with a sense.

The Rules of the Game

1. This is a game about the connections you make with colours, not the images that colours conjure up. So when you have your colour/sense combination, you must describe your thoughts and emotions rather than an image.

2. Give other players 30 seconds quiet time when they take their turn.

3. You may ask a friend to help you with the hearing sense, as this is the most difficult sense to connect.

Now you know what to do, let's get ready to share !

This game is all about having fun with your imagination. Go wild ! Have fun !

The Colour Share Game

CHAPTER FIVE

What's In A Rainbow ?

It's wonderful and magical to see a rainbow and all its colours.
But there's more to a rainbow than meets the eye.

Here comes the science bit...

Sir Isaac Newton was the greatest scientist of his time. He was born in England and lived from 1643-1727. He is best known for discovering the laws of gravity, but he also studied many other natural phenomena. In his efforts to understand more about the nature of light, he was working on some experiments at his home. One of his colour experiments went like this:

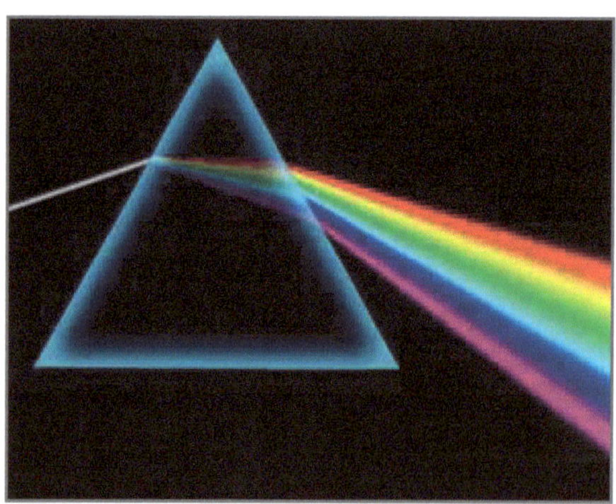

In his darkroom, he guided a shaft of sunlight to shine through a prism (a piece of glass). The light separated into the seven colours of the rainbow. Then he shone the separated light 'waves' into a second prism. This prism returned the light waves to their original stream of white light. The experiment showed that all the colours of the spectrum originate from white light. Although some people doubted Newton's conclusions at the time, it is now universally accepted as fact.

The Rainbow Poem

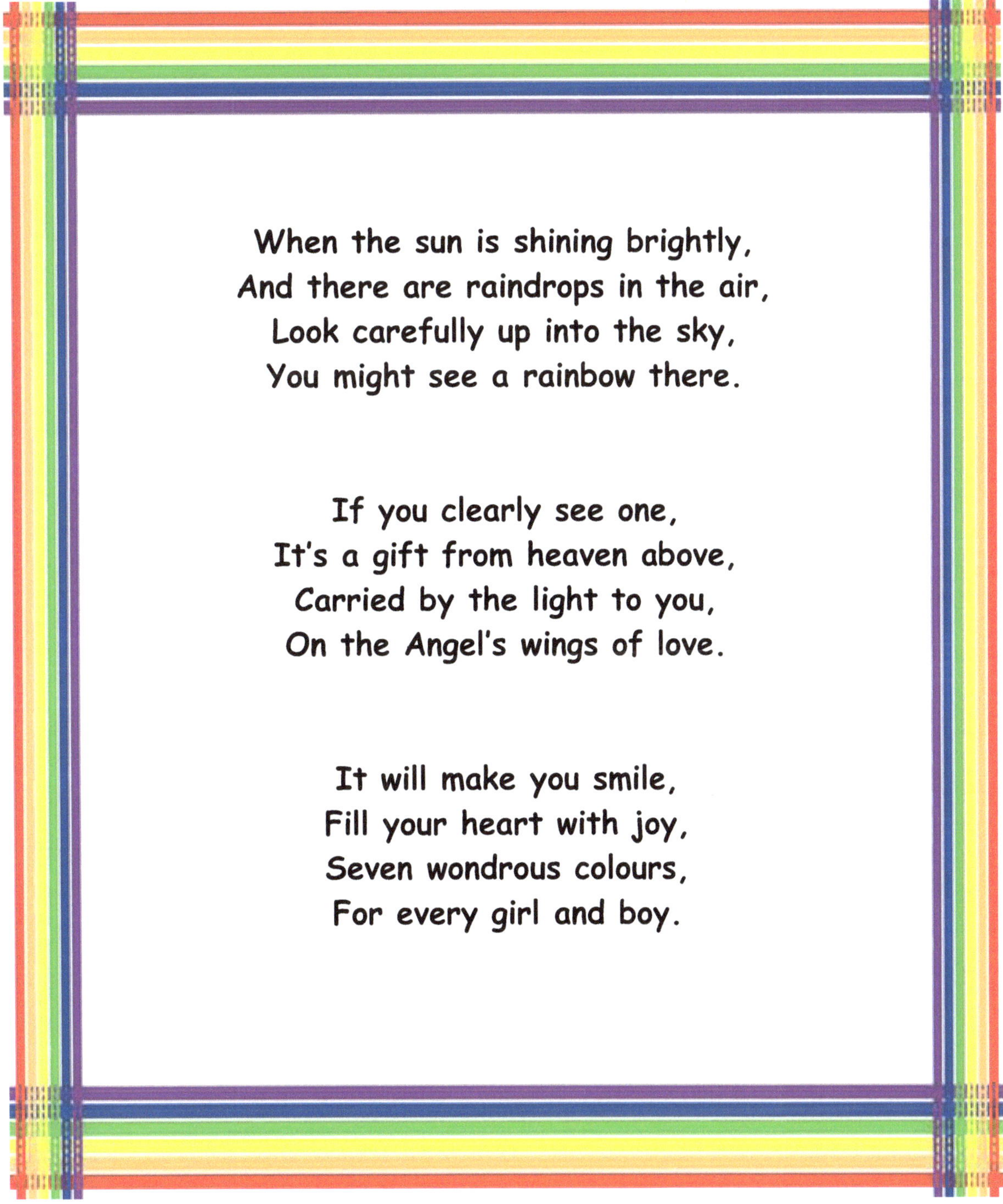

When the sun is shining brightly,
And there are raindrops in the air,
Look carefully up into the sky,
You might see a rainbow there.

If you clearly see one,
It's a gift from heaven above,
Carried by the light to you,
On the Angel's wings of love.

It will make you smile,
Fill your heart with joy,
Seven wondrous colours,
For every girl and boy.

The magic of the rainbow

Rainbows occur when water droplets and sunlight meet. The droplets act like tiny prisms. When the water droplets are large it is much easier to see a rainbow as the colours are stronger and clearer. There are many legends about the rainbow in different countries around the world. In Ireland, legend says that the leprechauns hide their pots of gold at the end of the rainbow.

All rainbows would be circular if the horizon of the earth didn't get in the way. If you're in an aeroplane, air balloon, ski lift or high up a mountain, look down and you might see a circular one.

The colours of the rainbow

Most people only see seven rays of colour and some less than seven, although there are actually many more.

If you look at the rainbow from the outside of the arc going in, the colours in order are:

Red, Orange, Yellow, Green, Blue, Indigo Violet.

In many cultures it is the symbol of hope, peace and harmony.

How to remember
the colours of the rainbow

If you can remember a silly sentence like the ones below, you'll be able to recite the colours of the rainbow in order.

Can you create your own silly sentence ? Here are some examples to help inspire you.

Riding **O**n **Y**our **G**ranny's **B**ike **I**n **V**enice.

Rockets **O**f **Y**ellow **G**oblins **B**last **I**nto **V**enus.

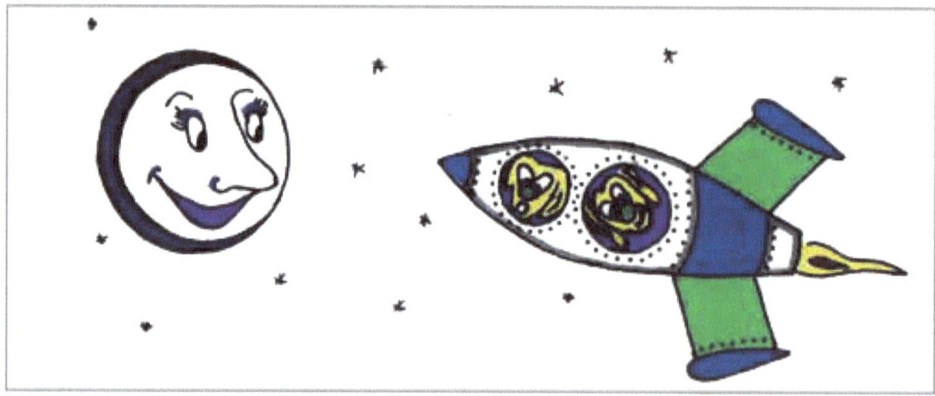

Write your own silly sentence here.

R............ O............ Y............ G............ B............ I............ V............

Double rainbows

Sometimes you may be lucky enough to see a double rainbow. If you do, you'll notice that the colours in the second rainbow are the other way around.

This is caused by a double reflection of sunlight inside the raindrop, like a mirror.

In between the first and secondary bow the area of the sky is darker. It is known as Alexander's Band, named after Alexander of Aphrodisias who first described this unlit area of the sky.

On very rare occasions several faint rainbows can be seen. It is called a supernumerary rainbow.

How to remember the colours of the rainbow backwards

Can you create a silly sentence to help remember the colour order backwards ?
Here are some examples to inspire you.

Vegetables **I**ncrease **B**eauty **G**row **Y**our **O**wn **R**adishes.

Very **I**nteresting **B**utterflies **G**oing **Y**onder **O**ver **R**ainbows.

Write your own silly sentence here.

V .... I .... B .... G .... Y .... O .... R ....

Where to see the colours of a rainbow

- On a soap bubble
- In the spray from a garden hose on a sunny day
- In the spray of a waterfall or an ocean wave
- In the winter sky, when it's foggy or misty
- In an oil patch on the road when it's been raining
- On a CD tilted towards the light
- In a crystal
- In a kaleidoscope
- When light passes through cut glass
- In a dew drop, early in the morning
- Images taken in deep space by the Hubble telescope
- In your mind - close your eyes and with the power of your imagination, picture a brightly coloured rainbow
- In a rainbow – of course !

Moonbow

Moonlight can produce rainbows at night time, just like sunlight causes rainbows during the day. They're called moonbows or lunar rainbows. Moonbows are not as easy to see as rainbows because moonlight is not very bright. You're more likely to see them when the moon is full. To see both rainbows and moonbows, the light always needs to be behind you.

The Rainbow in and around you

There is increasing evidence that when we are healthy and balanced a rainbow of colours shines out from within us in every direction like a diamond, moving and changing all the time.

Special cameras are used to take photographs of this colourful light show of energy, named by the ancients as an aura. The colours change according to the way we are thinking and feeling. Everyone's aura is different.

These auras or energy fields are not normally perceived by the regular five senses, but more and more people report being able to see them.

Many other forms of energy are not seen by the human eye, like radio waves and microwaves, but it doesn't mean that they don't exist.

Try to see if you can sense the energy of a friend.

Close your eyes and ask your friend to walk slowly towards you from any direction. Keeping your eyes closed, when you feel them getting close to you ask them to stop walking. Now guess if your friend is in front of you, behind you or to your side. You might be surprised how often you are right.

CHAPTER SIX

Colour Basics

How can you mix different tones of colours ? What colour goes with another ? Colour is easy when you know the basics.

Primary colours

Primary colours, or hues, are basic colours that can be mixed to make a whole range of other colours. There are specific sets of primary colours that are used for coloured lights, television, computer screens and printing. Red, green and blue are the primary hues of light. Projecting all three together will produce white light.
However, in art the three primary colours are different – they are traditionally red, yellow and blue. All other hues can be mixed from these three colours.

Other colours can't be mixed to make red, yellow and blue.

Just remember Ride Your Bike, and you will remember your primary colours.

Secondary colours

Mixing equal amounts of two primary colours together makes secondary colours. These are orange, green and purple.

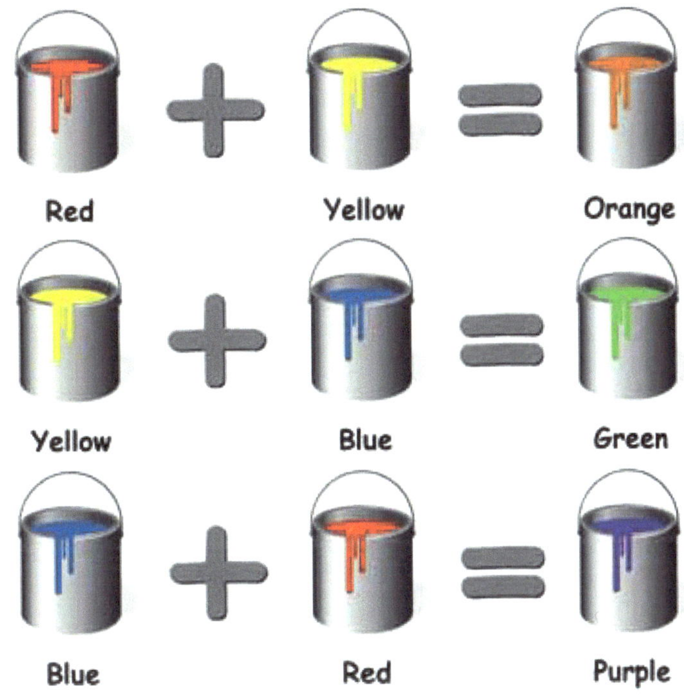

Try using paints to mix your own rainbow of colours.

Complementary colours

Johannes Itten's Colour Wheel

Complementary colours are directly opposite each other on a colour wheel. They make each other seem brighter and more alive. They look in harmony together and are often found in nature.
The colour wheel was developed by Johannes Itten in the 1920s. It represents the relationship between colours.

Red's complementary colour is green.

Blue's complementary colour is orange.

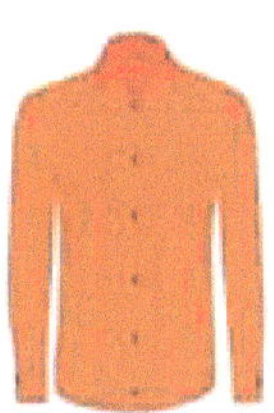

Yellow's complementary colour is violet.

Adjacent colours on the Colour Wheel – like blue and green or yellow and orange - also go well together. Tints and shades of the same hue such as purple and lavender or dark blue and light blue, look good too.

When choosing three different colours to wear, pick colours which are equally spaced out on the Colour Wheel in a triangle (triad). Examples include red, yellow and blue, lighter tints like pink, light blue and lemon and darker shades like purple, teal blue and brown.

All of your sign colours mix, match and blend well together because they all have the same undertones, so you can never go wrong.

Use this colour wheel and your inner senses to help you decide what colours to wear together – express yourself and look fantastic !

Changing the tone

The tone of a colour is changed by adding white or black to it. When you add white to a colour, it becomes lighter and is called a tint.

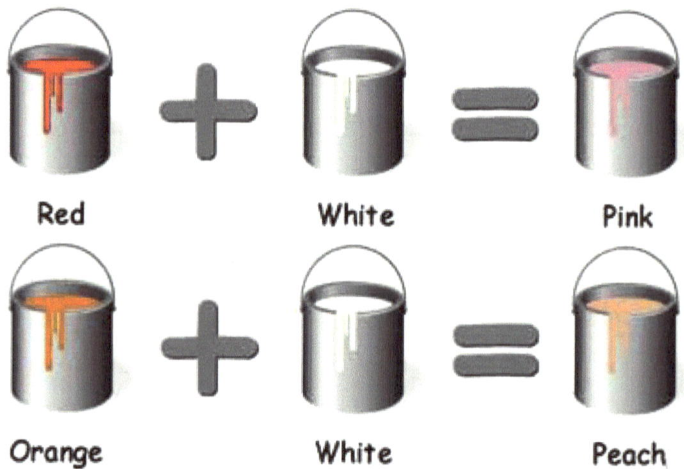

All of the other colours in the rainbow appear softer when white is added to them, so red becomes pink and orange becomes peach.

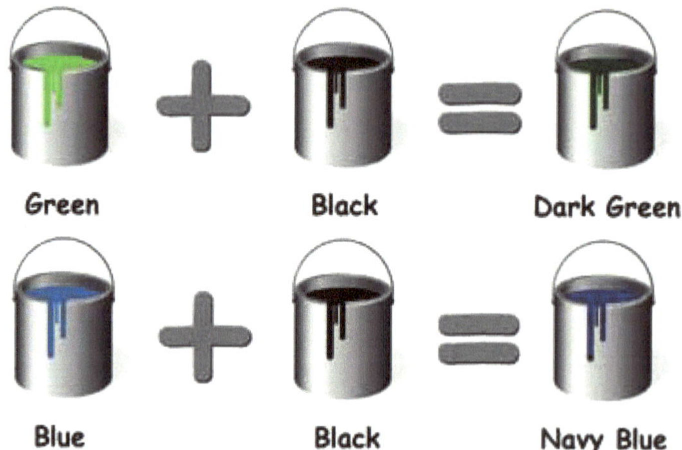

When black is added to a colour, it darkens and is called a shade. All colours appear deeper when black is added to them. For example, green changes to dark green, blue and black makes dark blue (navy). There are many different names to describe colours and new names appear every year. Names often relate to nature (sky blue), flowers (rose pink), birds (canary yellow) and food (tomato red).

CHAPTER SEVEN

Colour Clever

Most of the time we take colour for granted and don't tend to think about it.
Don't think about a pink elephant…

I bet you are now !

Colour Quiz

1. How many colours are there in a rainbow ?

2. Can you name them in the correct order ?

3. If you stare at the colour orange for a minute and then immediately look at plain white paper or a wall, what colour do you see ?

4. What colour is complementary and opposite to yellow ?

5. What two colours do you mix to make green ?

6. Can you guess what the world's favourite colour is ?

7. I'm a colour in the rainbow and you can eat me. What am I ?

8. Where do colours come from ?

Bonus question

Find the blue peace sign hidden somewhere in this book.

Turn to page 87 to discover the answers and see if you have passed with flying colours.

Did you know… ?

- There are many species in the Animal Kingdom which are able to change colour. This ability is used to scare away predators, attract a mate, communicate changing moods or disguise themselves whilst sneaking up on their prey.
The most well-known example is the chameleon.

- In Belgium the colour blue is considered to be a girl's colour and pink is more for boys.

- About 10 out of 100 boys have difficulty telling the difference between red and green. Some people can't see various shades of the same colour.

- Our spirits feel lifted and we feel more positive and healthy when we have been out in the sunshine because we have absorbed the spectrum of colours contained in the sunlight.

- Most of us are lucky enough to see in colour but did you know that some people with partial or no sight can actually identify colours by feeling the energy around them. Even people with good sight can learn this skill but it takes a lot of practice !

- 500 years ago poor people were forbidden to wear certain colours. Even today, certain religions do not allow women to wear brightly coloured clothes.

- Throughout history purple or violet (purple with white added to it) has been worn by kings, queens, cardinals and popes.

- Stinging insects prefer dark colours to light ones.

- Bees can't see the colour red, but can see ultraviolet - which is invisible to humans.

- In ancient Egypt it was thought that sick people could be cured by exposure to certain colours. Some temples were designed to allow pure or filtered sunlight to enter and be split into the colour spectrum. People who were ill were then placed under certain colours to restore them to health.

- Pink is the comforting colour that surrounded you when you were growing in your mother's womb. It is the colour of unconditional love.

- Dream experts say that if you dream in black and white you're dreaming about the past. If you dream in colour you are dreaming about the future.

- It's hard to relax or concentrate when you are in a brightly coloured room or wearing brightly coloured clothes because of the stimulating effect that strong colours have.

- Many theatres and television studios have a "Green Room". This is where actors and presenters can relax before performing on stage or in front of a camera.

- Most of us can see colours but some people can smell – or even taste – them ! This is a rare ability called synesthesia.

- For centuries colours have been used to describe emotions. If you're feeling blue you feel sad, if you see red you're angry and if you're green with envy then you're jealous.

- Many animals can only see in black and white.

Colour Questions and Activities

Questions

1. What is your favourite colour ? How does it make you feel ?
2. What is the first colour you see when you wake up in the morning ?
3. What is the colour of your favourite fruit ?
4. What was the colour of your favourite toy when you were very young ?
5. Have you got a favourite flower ? What colour is it ?
6. Is there a colour you don't like ? What is it ?

Sometimes we don't like a colour. Throughout our lives we connect colours with people, places, events and things that happen to us. So if we have a pleasant or unpleasant memory, it can affect the choice of colours we like.

Exercise your senses

Learn to develop your senses by concentrating on one sense at a time. You can do this anywhere, but it is more effective if you go somewhere close to nature where you can be amongst grass, trees and flowers. Now focus on a sense. If it's your sight, what details can you see in a flower ? What colours and shapes can you see in the

sky ? What do the patterns on the leaves look like ? What animals, birds or insects are you able to see ? What's the smallest thing you can see ? What's moving around you and in the distance ?
Focus in the same way with the other senses, but try closing your eyes to improve your concentration.

Time To Get Creative !

- Draw and colour your own flag or a flag of a country you'd like to visit in the box below.

- Imagine there is one flag for the whole world. Let's call it Planet Earth flag.
  Draw and colour in the flag the way you would like it to look.

Quiz answers

1) Seven colours

2) Red, orange, yellow, green,

   blue, indigo and violet

3) Blue

4) Purple

5) Yellow and blue

6) Blue

7) Orange

8) Light

Bonus
The answer is on page 44
2 points if you found it !

What's your total score ?

WELL DONE !

Colour yourself a gold star if you got them all correct.
If not, you can colour in the star with your favourite colour.

Word Search Puzzle

Have fun finding the colours of the rainbow, the four colour signs and the world in this tricky word search puzzle.
Words are hidden backwards, sideways, diagonally and upside down. You may like to ask a friend to help you. Good luck !
Tick the boxes next to the words below as you find them. To make it more fun you can highlight the colour words in the puzzle with a pen or pencil in the same colour.

N	P	H	D	M	S	N
H	T	R	A	E	O	O
O	E	U	L	B	R	O
W	L	O	V	E	A	M
D	O	G	I	D	N	I
N	I	L	L	S	G	N
U	V	R	L	A	E	D
S	O	N	E	E	R	G
W	O	R	G	S	Y	M

☐ Red
☐ Orange
☐ Yellow
☐ Green
☐ Blue
☐ Indigo
☐ Violet
☐ Sun
☐ Moon
☐ Sea
☐ Earth
☐ World

How many other words can you find ?

Answers are on **www.colourinmyworld.com**

Smile Day

We all feel good when we smile. Have a Smile Day with a friend or on your own.
Pick a day and wear your favourite colour. Smile every time you see anything or anyone in that colour. How many smiles can you gather in a day ?

Final Note:
I hope you've enjoyed reading this book as much as I've enjoyed writing it.
I'd like to invite you to visit my website:

www.colourinmyworld.com

You can post your own poem or picture, play games, share your own sentences about how to remember the colours of the rainbow and much, much more.

Let your colours shine. All my

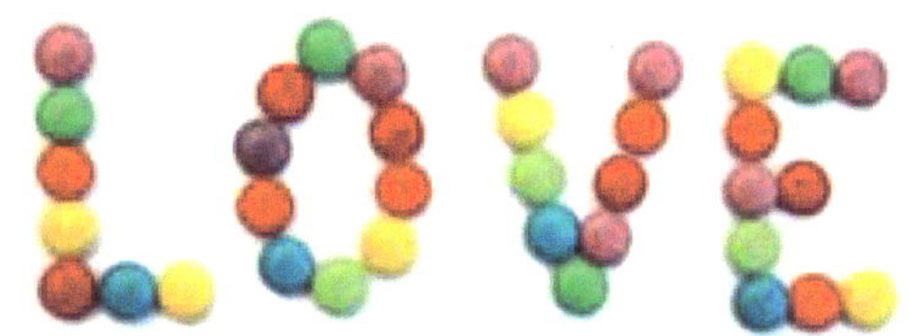

About the Author

Lynda Smith has spent the past thirty years helping people to feel great about themselves. She is a hair and make-up artist, colour/image consultant and Reiki practitioner. She has shared her knowledge through countless workshops, lectures and guest appearances on television and radio programmes. Lynda has a natural affinity with children and has combined her skills in writing Colour In My World, her first published book.

Acknowledgements

With enormous gratitude to my wonderful friend Tricia Essery, whose encouragement and enthusiasm motivated me to put pen to paper.
Website: internationalholisticcourses.com.

Geoff my husband and best friend, for his endless patience and support throughout the journey of this book.

Carlie my creative daughter who helped enormously with this book. Carlie is a person-centred counsellor and creative painting workshop facilitator.
Email: carlie-twigg@hotmail.co.uk.

Edward Murphy for his permission to use the aura photograph.
Email: edwardisis@msn.com.

Nick Hollings for his positive suggestions and proof reading.
Email: nechollings@gmail.com.

My friends and clients - you know who you are. "You are the colour in my world".